MAKE & FLY YOUR OWN ASIAN KITES

Easy Step-by-Step Instructions for 15 Colorful Kites

Asian kites

From the Thai Cobra to the Japanese Octopus

WAYNE HOSKING

TUTTLE Publishing

Tokyo | Rutland, Vermont | Singapore

Kite from Suruga

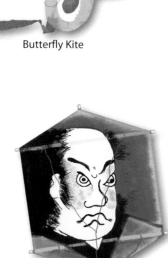

Octopus Kite

Butterfly Kite

Six-sided Kite

Contents

Buka Fighting Kite

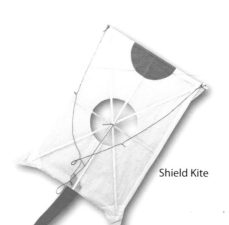

Shield Kite

Lark Kite

Thai Cobra Kite

Bug Kite

Spinning-top Kite

Mini Wau Kite

Sleeve Kite

Thai Fish Kite

Layang-layang Kite

Ray Fish Kite

Kites from Around the World

While watching your creation dancing on the wind, do you ever wonder who flew the first kite? Did the first kite come about by accident, by intentional design, or, as some cultures believe, as a "gift from the gods"? Even though the answer is lost in the distant past, scholars believe the existence of kites dates back to between two and a half to three thousand years ago. Ancient kites once carried messages—in the form of special shaped kites, pictures, or other cultural symbols—from earthbound humans to the heavenly beings in celebration of births, prosperity, and to ask for blessings. Over the centuries even common people began to fly kites, and everyday pleasure replaced the religious significance attached to kite flying.

Up until recent times, China received credit for developing the kite. This has been generally accepted because the Chinese had an advanced civilization that included the written word, allowing them to record historical events. The Chinese have a number of theories for the conception of the kite. On the top of the list is a legend about Meng Chia's bamboo hat being blown from his head by a sudden gust of wind. The farmer quickly raced after his hat, but was only able to grab an attached string. To his surprise, the hat kept on flying on its tether in the stiff breeze. The farmer enjoyed his flying hat and shared his discovery with the rest of his village.

A second theory begins with coastal villagers fascinated by large leaves blowing in the wind. They soon discovered that the wind could be harnessed by attaching lines to the leaves, producing a fun pastime. Even today, leaf kites exist in many parts of the world, from Indonesia to Japan.

A third theory claims that either a tent or sail became airborne in a strong wind, but remained

A bronze and pewter Chinese kite plaque by Philip LaVerne, New York. From the collection of Janet Hosking.

tethered by its lines. People who observed the phenomenon were able to reproduce the results of the accident in the form of a kite.

A fourth theory claims that kites came from man's desire to emulate birds—symbols of happiness and freedom—that hitched rides on local thermals. There is a Chinese tale about Mo Di (circa 400 b.c.), who spent three years perfecting his wooden bird-kite, called a muyuan, only to have it break after one day of flying.

Today, many kite enthusiasts believe that if materials and tools are the criteria for the development of the kite, then it is just as conceivable that kites originated in the region of the Malay Archipelago and adjoining Pacific Islands. Many of the Chinese theories for the discovery of the kite could just as easily have occurred in this part of the world. For example, since ancient islanders were renowned seamen, it is possible that kites originated from their experiences with sailing canoes. Also, their leaf and reed kites played roles in daily life, including fishing and making contact with the "spirit of the wind." Similar kites existed as far away as Hawaii and New Zealand.

The Polynesians explain the origin of the kite as a contest between Rango and Tan, two brothers who were also gods. According to legend, the brothers liked to challenge each other in sibling rivalry, and one day they decided to see who could fly a man-made bird the highest. Each constructed his kite from leaves and they met on the beach. However, the luckless Tan flew his kite too close to a tree and it became entangled. In the meantime, Rango's kite flew high and free. In celebration, Polynesians dedicate the highest-flying kites to the honor of Rango, the god of war and peace, death, and kite flying.

Perhaps the Malays, or Pacific Islanders, and the Chinese independently discovered how to

A leaf kite from Okinawa, Japan

make and fly kites, since there is little in common between the leaf and silk kites from these diverse regional cultures. However, it is possible to notice similarities between a later Chinese fertility kite and the Malaysian wau, such as an association with the fertility of rice fields. These similarities may be coincidental or may have resulted from later contacts between the two regions.

Though the birthplace of the kite is a little unclear, the Chinese can at least take credit for spreading kites to the four corners of the world through trade. Stories of Chinese kite flying finally reached Europe in the thirteenth century, courtesy of Marco Polo, a Venetian trader and adventurer.

In the sixteenth and seventeenth centuries, Europeans found a sea route around the Cape of Good Hope and into the East Indies and China. These early traders brought back to Europe examples of kites that became children's toys and objects of curiosity. However, by the eighteenth and nineteenth centuries, Europeans and Americans were using kites as tools for scientific studies of the natural elements, including developing flying machines. In the meantime, Asians were still flying kites to celebrate nature and the human spirit.

Today, Asian countries still keep in touch with their past and culture through kite festivals. Kite associations share their culture with new generations and the rest of the world. Many of the associations organize kite tours and look forward to receiving international visitors.

Flying kites with your friends is much more fun!

Making Your Own Asian Kites

Kite making can be a satisfying and fun experience for all ages. Once you know the basic terms and materials used, and how it all goes together properly, you will have a fun and uplifting experience. Further, all who gaze upon your flying creations can then share the results.

Materials and Parts of a Kite

Kites can be made of almost any material, from thin, veneered wood to feathers, as long as the wind is strong enough to lift the kite's weight and the kite is aerodynamic—that is, it has a special shape allowing the object to fly. Asians traditionally make their kites from handmade paper and bamboo. However, bamboo is not readily available in the West and is hard to work with, and handmade paper tends to be expensive and so is mainly used in art in our part of the world. Consequently, the time-honored designs in this book feature materials readily available at craft and hobby shops or on the Internet. If you would like to use traditional materials, then adjustments may need to be made to the design to account for weight and flexibility. Just remember when choosing your materials that the heavier a kite is, the harder it is to fly, because excessive weight tends to make a kite unstable.

THE FRAME
(also called the spars or bones)

By supporting the sail, the frame helps form and keep the kite's shape.

BASSWOOD or SPRUCE flat sticks make excellent kite spars because of their flexibility, strength, and weight. Basswood spars are available from craft and hobby shops.

BALSAWOOD can also be used, but best suits small kites, for which weight, and not strength, is critical.

BAMBOO is the spar material of choice for Asian kites because of its availability and high ratio of strength to weight. Bamboo is generally available whole, but most small kites require only split-bamboo sticks. Matchstick bamboo window shades can be dismantled to make kite spars for small kites. Bamboo and window shades are available from specialty stores.

DOWEL is an all-around spar material that is available at lumberyards and hardware and hobby shops.

THE SAIL
(also called the cover or skin)

The sail attaches to the frame, forming the surface that catches and deflects the wind so that the kite will fly.

PAPER is easy to work with and to decorate, but it does not hold up to rough treatment or moisture. If you find that you do not have a sheet of paper big enough to cover the whole kite, then it is possible to glue sections of paper together until they create the right size.

SILKSPAN is a tissue used by hobbyists to cover model aircraft. It is stronger than regular tissue, but will shrink if it becomes wet, which can be a negative or positive quality, depending on how it is used. For example, I painted the wings of my Lark kite, but left some parts of the wing alone, which created a three-dimensional effect. Silkspan comes in three weights—light, medium, and heavy—and is available from hobby shops.

TISSUE PAPER is excellent for making kites to fly in light wind. Tissue paper is available in different weights and colors from hobby and art supply stores, and is also available in the form of gift-wrapping paper.

JAPANESE MULBERRY (Washi or Kozo) AND CHINESE RICE PAPER are traditional kite-making papers. These specialty papers are often relatively expensive and are available from art supply stores in white and off-white, and man-made or machine-made. Mulberry paper is available in different weights. For kites, look for something in the weight range of bond paper (approximately 40 gm/sq m).

TYVEK® is a spun-bonded polyethylene (plastic-like) material made by DuPont (synthetic paper version is known as type #10; the soft cloth version is type #14). Tyvek® is almost indestructible and can take gluing, sewing, printing, and painting. The disadvantage of Tyvek® is its flight characteristics. The paper version tends to be stiff and not bend as well as paper does in the wind, and this can cause the kite to be unstable, a negative effect usually overcome with the addition of more tail. Tyvek® is available from kite material suppliers and building suppliers, since Tyvek® is also used to wrap insulate houses. For use in smaller

Tools Needed for Making Kites

Most tools for making kites are simple and can usually be found around the home.

SCISSORS: for cutting sails

NEEDLE: large, blunt type, for threading the bridle

YARDSTICK OR RULER: for measuring and drawing lines

PEN OR PENCIL: for drawing the pattern and marking the kite sail

GLUE STICK: for gluing sail

WHITE GLUE: for gluing spars together

TAPE: preferably clear tape, for reinforcing and repairs

KITE STRING: for bridles

POSTER BOARD: for sail pattern

SMALL SAW: for sawing spars

WOOD BLOCK: for a sawing or cutting surface

REPAIR KIT FOR THE FIELD

STRING

TAPE

TAIL

SMALL SCISSORS

GLUE

SPARS (SHORT LENGTHS OF WOOD TO USE AS SPLINTS)

kites, you may wish to use Tyvek® envelopes, available through the U.S. Postal Service.

CREPE PAPER best suits kite tails or decorative elements. You should be aware that the colors tend to "bleed" from crepe paper when it becomes wet. I once had a classroom full of rainbow-colored children after flying kites in a wet schoolyard!

WRAPPING PAPER, BROWN KRAFT PAPER, AND NEWSPAPER are all traditional covering material for kites in the West, but they also tend to be heavy (note that weight can cause a kite to spin) and they also tear easily.

THE KITELINE
(also called the cord or tether)

The kite line is held by the kite flier and attaches to the kite so it will fly. Early Asian kite fliers fashioned their lines from silk and other natural fibers. Even today, traditional Japanese kite fliers use line made from hemp or flax. Others use synthetic line, such as nylon or polyester, because of the cost and strength advantage over the traditional line material.

Your choice of line will directly influence how your kite flies. A heavy line tends to pull a kite down; a light line has the risk of breaking. Fuzzy-textured line, such as cotton and linen, will catch the wind, causing a kite to fly in one direction while the line pulls in another. To lessen this effect, known as drag, some fliers wax their line with beeswax. *Avoid using clear fishing line and wire* because they can be extremely dangerous. I recommend using #10 crochet thread or buttonhole thread for small kites.

Use a fishing swivel at the tow point, the point where the kite line attaches to the kite, to remove twists from your line and to make it easier to disconnect the kite line. However, use a swivel that is equal to the kite line's strength, because a heavy swivel will weigh a kite down.

THE LINE WINDER
(also called the reel)

The line winder holds the kite line. There is no best kind of winder. Traditional Indian, Japanese, and Korean kite winders are simple, but very effective, handheld reels. Some Japanese kite fliers use woven baskets to hold their line. Some people in the West use a stick or a short length of a broom handle around which to wind their line in a figure-eight fashion, or they use a rod and reel.

One of the most economical line winders is a soup can with one end removed. Electric or duct tape applied around the inside rim can protect your fingers from any sharp edges. In addition, a pet-food resealing lid, sold in supermarkets and pet stores, will both protect fingers and can double as a container for a first aid kit for the flying field described earlier.

THE TAIL

The main purpose of the tail is to add drag, but not weight. A good tail should act as a stabilizer and not throw the kite off balance. Three materials recommended for a kite tail are strips of paper glued together, strips of cloth, or crepe paper. To attach a tail to your kite, simply glue or tape the tail end to the kite sail.

The kite tail is often an afterthought, but on many kites it can be an important component. If you are unsure of what length to make the tail, a simple rule of thumb is to use a tail seven times the length of the sail of the kite. Too much tail will create excessive drag, causing a kite to pull to one side or even refuse to fly. The drag factor of a tail can be increased or reduced by changing the tail length or by adding strips to the end of the tail, called a ponytail. Usually, the stronger the wind is, the more tail required. In addition, to increase drag, you can try a material with more wind resistance. I carry a roll of crepe paper for this purpose.

Attaching streamers to the sides of a kite can create extra stability, since they control any snaking, side-to-side motion, called *yaw*. If a kite is off balance and pulls to one side, add a piece of kite tail to the opposite side.

Instead of a tail, Japanese traditional kite fliers use rope as a stabilizer on larger kites. When the kite tries to veer off course, the line tends to lessen the motion.

THE BRIDLE

The bridle is the line or lines (called bridle legs) that sets the kite to the wind. It is located between the kite's sail and the kite line and attaches to the kite at the bridle points. The point where the kite line attaches to the bridle is called the tow point.

Because there is no standard bridle, you should use the style that best suits the kite. Some bridles may require adjustments for various wind conditions; some kites have the kite line attached directly to the kite at a single tow point and no bridle; others may have up to hundreds of bridle legs. By using multiple bridles, it is possible to use thinner or more flexible spars. The lighter a kite is, the easier it is to fly it. Many Asian kites come without bridles so that the fliers can make the kite their own by bridling them.

It is very easy to make a bridle. You will need a tape measure or ruler, a marking pen, and bridle line. Using the measurements given in this book, mark the tow point and the tie points on the line—the given length of the bridle. Before cutting the line, allow an extra 2" (50 mm) at each end for tying.

To attach the bridle to the kite, pass the line through the sail with a needle or crochet hook at the bridle point, shown with small circles in the kite diagrams. To complete the process, tie the bridle ends around the spars or spine at the marked points on the bridle line.

If you ever make a kite where there is no bridle information given, you do not have to be an aeronautical engineer or do many calculations to come up with the correct bridle length. As a rule of thumb, a bridle should be one and a half

to three times the length of the kite. If you use a short bridle, the tow point will become very critical; a long bridle is more tolerant of various tow points.

A bridle should support the kite spars, distorting them only to add stability to the kite. Add extra bridle legs to carry the load if the spars distort too much, or if there is a risk that the wind pressure will break the spars. On smaller kites, it might just require relocating the bridle points.

THE TOW POINT

The tow point—the point of connection between the bridle and the kite line—sets the kite at the correct angle to the wind, often called the *angle of attack*, and is crucial because the kite will not fly right if the kite line is not connected at the correct point. A tow point set at a high angle allows wind to pass by the kite. If the tow point is set too high, the kite will tend to be an unstable flier.

A tow point set at a low angle allows the kite to catch and deflect most of the wind. If the tow point is too low, however, the kite will not deflect the wind and it will refuse to fly. Another effect of a too-low tow point is that the kite will pull to one side, as it tries to let loose the trapped wind.

One method of setting the tow point is to take the kite outdoors and hold it by the bridle in the wind. Move your fingers along the bridle until the kite seems to want to fly. This is the correct tow point. Another method is to hold the bridle at a potential tow point and make a figure eight in the air. If the kite follows along, then the tow point is correct. With either method, though, you may have to adjust the tow point when flying the kite a second time.

A Japanese technique for locating the correct tow point is to start by gathering all the bridle legs at a predetermined set point, usually found by trial and error, on the kite. Move your hand along the bridle and tie a loop at the end, creating a tow point.

KNOTS

There are only three knots that the novice kite maker should learn. The knots are so simple that it is more than likely that you already know them. They are a Lark's Head (an adjustable hitch), a Loop, and a Square Knot. Remember that a poorly tied knot can result in damage to or loss of your kite. Synthetic lines, such as nylon or polyester, can be difficult to tie into knots because the material tends to be slippery. To prevent the knot from slipping, tie a figure-eight knot at the line end.

Constructing Your Kite

After selecting the design of your kite, use a material such as poster board to make a pattern for the sail. The kite's instructions will explain if you will need to make a whole or half pattern. An advantage of a pattern is that it allows you to check all the kite's measurements before making the actual kite.

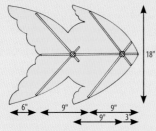

In addition, having a ready-made pattern makes it easier to build future versions. After making the pattern, trace the sail outline onto the paper and cut it out. You might consider decorating the kite sail at this point, or you can wait until the kite is finished.

Cut spars to the correct length, after checking the measurements. Remember: Measure twice and cut once! Apply glue to the length of the spars and glue the spars to the sail. A glue stick is best for this process because its glue will not damage a thin tissue sail; liquid glues tend to melt fragile paper. Applying a spot of white glue to the spars at their intersection points will create extra stability.

When possible, run a length of line around the outside of the frame, called a framing line, to protect and support the edges of the sail. However, because many of the kites in this book are so small and their edges are not square, this step can often cause more problems than it can resolve. Clear tape can also reinforce unprotected edges. Finally, reinforce the sail by applying paper patches over the ends of the spars.

An alternative to adding extra tail to stabilize a kite is to bow the cross spars. Bowing the spars increases the wind pressure to any side that dips and throws a kite off balance, which in turn brings the kite back to stable flight. If the instructions call for a bowed spar, tie a line (called a bowline) at both ends of the spar, carefully bow the spar, and wind any excess line around the spar end.

Decorating Your Kite

Be aware that in most Asian cultures, a plain white kite is a symbol of sorrow. When decorating a kite, keep your designs large and bold because small, intricate work will be lost in the viewing distance. To test how a kite will look, place it against a wall and view it from across the room.

Paints and Inks

In Japan, traditional kite makers use colorful dyes to paint their kites. However, for the Western kite maker, most artists' ink will produce similar results. If used sparingly, wide-tipped marker pens are excellent for decorating a kite's tissue sails. However, I do not recommend using water paints on tissue paper sails because the water will dissolve the paper.

If you are searching for imaginative ideas, try looking through children's coloring books or stained glass designs. You will find that simple artwork works well on a kite. In addition, books on Asian art or quilting are excellent resources for designs.

Ink stamps and color pens are one of the simplest methods for young children to decorate a kite, and they will not create any weight or balance problems.

PAPER CUTOUTS

Using paper cutouts is a traditional method of decorating kites in many parts of the world. For example, Malaysian kite makers use multiple layers of different colored, intricately cut paper to decorate their wau. The method most commonly used in other parts of the world is to fold the paper and cut the desired pattern or shape before gluing it to the sail. Overlaying different colored pieces of tissue paper can create special effects. For a bold effect, use colorful Japanese origami paper. However, you have to be mindful of the extra added weight and the risk of throwing the kite off balance.

NOISEMAKERS

An important part of many traditional Asian kites is a device that will flap or vibrate in the wind to create a melodic sound. One belief is that the "music" attracts the attention of the heavenly gods.

To make a hummer, bow a length of spar with a strip of metallic curling ribbon as the bowstring to create the vibrator. The bows of traditional Japanese hummers use bamboo and thin strips of rattan for the vibrator. Also, gluing a strip of paper to the bowline creates a "buzzer."

Setting Up a Work Area

When making kites, it is important to set up a special place to work. A work area can be anywhere, like a table, desk, or even the floor. Because the kite maker will be using glue, it is advisable to have a plastic sheet underneath, such as a large trash bag, to protect the work area during the kite's construction.

Kite Storage and Transporation

The main problem with most Asian kites is that they do not fold or roll up for storage or transportation, which makes them easy to damage. To solve the problem, I recommend creating your very own kite portfolio or transporter. For my own kite collection, I use an artist's portfolio available from arts and craft stores.

MAKING A KITE CARRIER

A kite portfolio is a kite carrier that is inexpensive and simple to make. It is very useful for transporting your kites without damaging them. For example, cardboard can be cut from a large cardboard box, or purchased from a shipping center or craft store.

What You Need

- Two pieces of cardboard or ⅛"-thick (3 mm) plywood sheet, larger than kite
- Tape (duct or packaging tape)

How to Make the Portfolio

1 Hinge the two pieces of board by taping them together along their long edges.

2 Fold the boards together and tape the outside of the hinged edge.

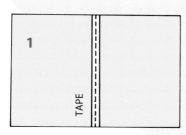

Flying Your Kites

Learning to fly a kite is like riding a bike: Once you learn how, it is hard to forget. Because there are a few simple rules to follow when flying a kite, it is advisable to understand this section of the book before heading out to the wide-open spaces.

When to Fly a Kite

The traditional kite-flying season is in the spring. Nevertheless, winds at this time of year can be too strong and gusty for most paper kites. When tree branches are tossing about, many people mistakenly call it "kite weather." If you fly in gusting winds, you risk damage or even the loss of your kite. Furthermore, if there is a thunderstorm in your area, leave your kite at home, because kite line will conduct electricity, a fact proven by Ben Franklin's very dangerous experiment. Also, watch the birds: If they are having a difficult time flying, then it is advisable not to fly a kite. If the conditions are right, and the wind is within the recommended wind range, you can fly your kite at any time of the year.

Wind Strength

In addition to your running, the wind provides the energy needed to fly a kite. Each kite in this book lists a recommended wind range in which it is safe to fly the kite. The best way to determine the wind strength is to use the following wind scale and observe nearby trees, smokestacks, large bodies of water, or flags.

How to Fly Your Kite

A kite is most at risk for breakages when flown for the first time (and while being carried to the flying field). Before launching your kite, check the bridle, tow point, knots, kite symmetry, and the condition of your kite line. Watch carefully and note how the kite first reacts to the wind. Run forward so that the kite can land safely if it starts to spin or fly in an erratic fashion. Also, refer to the troubleshooting section of this book for helpful hints on how to correct your kite.

Where to Fly Your Kite

Try to fly in an open area away from power lines, trees, buildings, roadways, and airports. Also, try to imagine what may happen if the wind changes direction. The golden rule of kite flying is to fly only where the kite will not create a hazard to you or others. Beaches, parks, open fields, and schoolyards are generally the best flying areas.

Once you have chosen a location, you will next need to watch out for nearby trees, buildings, or terrain that can spoil the wind quality. It may feel as if the wind is blowing in one direction when in fact it is merely rolling around an obstruction, creating ground turbulence, often called the

Launching a Kite Alone by Yourself

It is easier to launch a kite with help from another person, but if you ever want to fly alone, here are a few tips. Let out some line and, with your back to the wind, point the kite upward. Hold the kite away from your body so that you do not block the wind. When the wind catches the kite, slowly pump on the line by pulling it back and forth, and let out more line. Do not pull hard, because this will usually cause the kite to dive. Keep feeding out line until the kite reaches the desired altitude. Do not let the line run rapidly through your fingers, since you may receive a burn or cut.

Many people feel that running with a kite is part of kite flying, but this can be a dangerous practice. When running, it is difficult to watch both the kite's action and for obstacles that may result in a damaged kite or personal injury.

Launching With an Assistant

Your assistant should be downwind 50 to 100 feet (15 to 30 meters), holding the kite with the kite line taught. On a given signal, have the kite launched with a slight upward push. As the kite rises, pump on and release more line.

wind shadow. Turbulence can make it difficult to launch and fly a kite. To better understand a flying area, watch the action and direction of flags, trees, or smoke. They will generally indicate by blowing in different directions whether there is a disturbed wind flow. Another indication of turbulent air will be that a kite that normally flies well will pull to one side or fly in an erratic fashion. If a kite can reach an altitude above the turbulence, it will most likely settle down to stable flying. Therefore, if turbulence is a problem, try a high launch or another location. When flying near a wind obstruction, use a ratio of one to five: If a tree is 30 feet (10 meters) tall, stay at least 150 feet (50 meters) downwind.

Troubleshooting Tips

Understanding this section can often make the difference between fun under the sun and a very disappointed kite flier. Troubleshooting actually starts at the very beginning of your kite project. By using the correct materials, and carefully following the instructions, you can avoid many of the potential pitfalls.

Do not use a spar with a diameter different

Wind Scale

LIGHT AIR: 2–3 mph (3–5 km/h)
Smoke drifts and flags show little movement; ripples on water.

LIGHT BREEZE: 4–7 mph (6–11 km/h)
Leaves rustle and flags flutter; small wavelets form.

GENTLE BREEZE: 8–12 mph (12–19 km/h)
Flags fly and leaves dance; waves crest.

MODERATE BREEZE: 13–18 mph (20–29 km/h)
Trees toss and dust flies; white caps form.

FRESH WIND: 19–24 mph (30–39 km/h)
Small trees sway; moderate waves form with some spray.

STRONG WIND: 25–31 mph (40–49 km/h)
Large branches sway; large waves form with foam crests.

from what is recommended. The weight of thicker spars can cause a kite to spin; thinner spars can cause bucking or even break. Flexible spars can sometimes be beneficial to a kite's stability by bending to instead of fighting the wind, but they need the correct bridle.

Keep your kite line clear of knots and nicks. A knot can weaken a line up to thirty percent.

IF THE KITE SPINS EVEN THOUGH THE WIND IS NOT VERY STRONG:

- Check the tail, which could be too short.
- Check that the spars fit correctly and the sides of the kites are equal.
- Lower the tow point along the bridle.
- Bow the cross spar.
- Add tails to the sides of the kite.
- Add extra bridle legs to control how the spars bend.

IF THE KITE FAILS TO LAUNCH AND THE WIND IS STRONG ENOUGH FOR THE KITE:

- Check the tail, which could be too heavy.

- Raise the tow point, along the bridle.
- Add extra bridle legs if the spars are too flexible.

IF THE KITE PULLS OR DIPS TO ONE SIDE:

- Raise the tow point, along the bridle.
- Remove a section of tail.
- Tape a kite tail to the side opposite of the dipping.
- Try a different flying area.

IF THE KITE MOVES IN A SIDE-TO-SIDE MOTION:

- Add side tails.
- Move the tow point backward or forward along the bridle.

IF THE KITE MAKES A BUCKING MOTION:

- Replace or stiffen the spine, or bow the spars.
- Add extra bridle legs.

Safety Code

NEVER FLY YOUR KITE NEAR POWER LINES. If a kite tangles in power lines, LEAVE IT THERE and notify the local utility company of the situation.

FLY ONLY WHERE THE KITE WILL NOT CREATE A HAZARD TO YOU OR OTHERS. Fly kites in flat, open areas away from buildings and roadways.

NEVER FLY A KITE DURING AN APPROACHING STORM.

ALWAYS OBSERVE LOCAL AIR SAFETY REGULATIONS AND AVOID FLYING IN AIR TRAFFIC PATTERNS CLOSE TO AIRPORTS.

DO NOT LET LINE RUN THROUGH THE FINGERS AT A FAST RATE, BECAUSE THIS WILL RESULT IN A BURN OR CUT.

DO NOT USE BLADES OR SHARP, POINTED OBJECTS ON A KITE OR LINE.

DO NOT THROW HEAVY OBJECTS AT AN ENTRAPPED KITE. TRY TO HAVE THE KITE FLY ITSELF FREE, EVEN IF IT MEANS CUTTING YOUR LINE.

DO NOT LEAVE A KITE FLYING UNATTENDED, ESPECIALLY NEAR ROADWAYS.

Kites from China

Many historians believe that China, one of the three cradles of civilization, is the birthplace of the kite. Their evidence rests mainly in the existence of the earliest written account of kite flying, dating back to 196 B.C.E. The description revealed how the Chinese general Han Hsin had a kite flown above a besieged stronghold to calculate the distance that his army would have to tunnel to get there. When the kite flew over the impregnable wall, the troops marked the kite line. Knowing the distance to dig, the troops were able to excavate a tunnel under the wall to surprise their enemy and become victorious.

Another legend from the Han Dynasty (A.D. 25–220) revealed how Han Hsin defeated a general named Hsiang Yu. Han ordered his troops to fly giant kites equipped with noisemakers over Hsiang's camp at night. The encamped enemy thought that the eerie sound was made by guardian angels warning of impending doom, and so they fled in terror.

Kites did not always create the desired solution, as with besieged Emperor Liang. In desperation, the emperor offered a reward to anyone who could send a message to his troops waiting in another county. A servant thought that a message-carrying kite would be the best answer. However, the kite fell short of its mark, thus allowing the emperor's enemy to learn of his troubled state, which led to his eventual demise.

Besides for military purposes, the Chinese flew kites with cultural and religious significance. The invention of paper by Tsai Lun during the eastern Han Dynasty allowed kites to become a universal folk art and made it possible for all people to enjoy kite flying. In one Chinese province, participants running through open fields while flying kites ruined farmers' crops to such an extent that a law was enacted to outlaw the pastime!

In the northern Sung Dynasty (A.D. 960–1126), kites gained great popularity and became a source of amusement for all ages. A festival called Kite Day was celebrated on the ninth day of the ninth month of every year. A story of the origin of this festival tells of a man called Haun Ching. A fortuneteller told Haun that on the ninth day of the ninth month a calamity would befall his household. To secure his family's safety, he followed the fortuneteller's advice to take them to the hills on that day to drink chrysanthemum wine and fly kites. Having done what he was told, he returned home to find all his farm animals dead. In remembrance of the event, people continued to travel to the hills, taking their kites. In time, the people believed that they avoided a whole year's bad luck by flying kites. A kite flown at a high altitude would reach the "spirit world" and carry away all the ill fate of the earthbound mortal.

One of the oldest Chinese kite traditions is associated with the spring festival of Ching Ming.

As part of the festivities, families visited the graves of their ancestors to pay respect and to worship. By flying kites, the partakers believed they could scare away any evil spirits lurking at the grave sites.

In the thirteenth century, Marco Polo, a Venetian trader and adventurer, described an incident in which a man was bound to a large kite that Polo called a "hurdle," and it was flown to see "whether its business will go well or ill on that voyage." If the kite failed to fly, then the ship would not have made the voyage.

During the Ging Dynasty (1644–1911), it became popular practice to fly and release a kite to take away one's bad luck and illness. By getting the participants outdoors and into the sunshine and fresh air, this result of kite flying may have been unavoidable! Also, another superstition stated that a found kite placed under a chamber pot overnight would take away any evil.

Today, China is famous for six main kite regions: Beijing, Weifang, Tianjin, Nantong, Jiangnan, and Taiwan. Each region uses a unique kite style, with more than three hundred types of kites. *Feng-zheng* ("wind harp" in Mandarin dialect) is the generally accepted term for Chinese kites, but they are also known by many other names, depending on the region and period. In Mandarin dialect, a kite can also be a *zhi-yuan* ("paper kite"), and in Cantonese dialect, a *fun-tsun* or a *pianzi*.

Because kite flying is a folk tradition, its practice closely follows local customs and growing seasons, and October is the traditional month for kite flying. However, because of favorable winds, the main kite-flying season usually runs for another three months, from the Chinese New Year (late January or early February) through Qingming, the day for mourning the dead, which falls on April 5 and corresponds with the onset of warmer weather, the start of spring plowing, and family outings.

PROJECT 1:
Butterfly Kite

Recommended for ages 9–12

The Butterfly Kite is a fair to good flier in light to gentle breezes. The Chinese often make and fly Butterfly kites because they represent beauty and a free spirit. There is an old saying: Only the greatest artists go to heaven to paint butterfly wings.

What You Need

SAIL: one 21" (535 mm)-square piece of medium-weight Silkspan

SPARS:
- one 11" (355 mm) x ¼" (6 mm) x ¹⁄₁₆" (2 mm) piece of basswood, for the spine
- two 24" (635 mm) x ¼" (6 mm) x ¹⁄₁₆" (2 mm) pieces of basswood, for the top spars
- two 12" (330 mm) x ¼" (6 mm) x ¹⁄₁₆" (2 mm) pieces of basswood, for the bottom spars

BRIDLE: 24" (610 mm) piece of kite line

REINFORCING LINE (OPTIONAL): piece of kite line

TAIL: two 48" (1220 mm) x 1½" (40 mm) paper streamers

GLUE AND PAPER PATCHES

PATTERN MATERIAL: heavy paper or cardboard

KITE LINE: #20 kite line (available at kite stores)

ANTENNAE (OPTIONAL): two wire twist ties from trash bags, or a pipe cleaner

Making the Kite

1

After making a pattern of half of the kite, fold the sail in half and trace the pattern onto the sail, with the kite center along the fold. Allow a ½" (12 mm) glue flap along the top edge. Cut out the sail and snip at 2" (50 mm) intervals along the gluing flap.

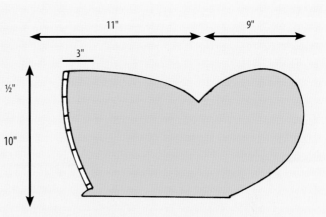

2

Glue the spine to the sail. Starting with one top corner, glue the flap over the spar and let the glue set for a moment. Bend the spar and, using a paper patch, glue the other end to the sail. Finish gluing the other corner of the top flap. Repeat the same steps for the other spar.

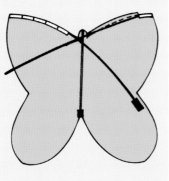

3

Glue the bottom spars to the sail and finish them with paper patches.

OPTIONAL: Run a reinforcing line between the spars.

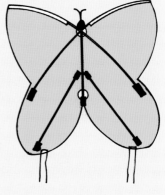

4

Use a blunt needle to thread the bridle through the sail at the given bridle points. Tie the ends of the bridle around the spars at the bottom bridle point.

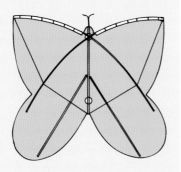

5

Measure and tie the kite line at the tow point. Glue tails to the sail.

OPTIONAL: Tape or glue the antennae to the butterfly's head.

PROJECT 2:
Lark Kite

Recommended for ages 9–12

The Lark Kite is a fair to good flier in light to gentle breezes. In China, birds are a symbol of happiness and kept for their beauty and singing ability.

What You Need

SAIL: one 18" (455 mm) x 24" (610 mm) piece of medium-weight Silkspan

SPARS:
- one 18" (455 mm) x ¼" (6 mm) x ¹⁄₁₆" (2 mm) piece of basswood, for the spine
- one 24" (610 mm) x ¼" (6 mm) x ¹⁄₁₆" (2 mm) piece of basswood, for the top spar
- two 4" (100 mm) x ⅛" (3 mm) x ¹⁄₁₆" (2 mm) pieces of basswood, for the tail spreaders

(**NOTE:** cut a length of ¼" [6 mm] basswood scrap in half with your scissors)

PATTERN MATERIAL: heavy paper or cardboard

BRIDLE: 36" (915 mm) piece of kite line

TAIL: three 36" (1 meter) x 1" (25 mm) paper streamers

GLUE AND PAPER PATCHES

KITE LINE: #10 crochet thread

Making the Kite

1

Draw a grid of 1½" (40 mm) squares on pattern material and draw half of the kite. Cut out the pattern. Fold the sail in half and trace the pattern onto the sail with the pattern centered on the fold. Allow a 4" (100 mm) x ½" (12 mm) glue flap at the ends of the top edges.

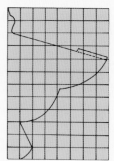

1 square = 1½"

2

Unfold the sail and glue the spine along the fold. Fold the glue flap and glue the spar to sail, slightly bowing the spar.

3

Glue the tail spreaders to the sail and glue the paper patches over the spine and spreader ends.

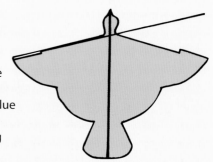

23"

6"
9½"

12"

4

Use the blunt needle to thread the bridle through the sail at the given bridle points. Tie the ends of the bridle around the spar at the top bridle point, and the spine at the bottom bridle point. Measure and tie the bridle to the kite line at the tow point. Glue a single tail to the sail and glue the other two tails to the bottom of the first tail.

16"

16½"

Kites from Malaysia

Malaysians have flown kites for so long that many modern scholars believe the Malay Archipelago may have been the actual birthplace of the kite. Further, Malaysians are spiritual and peace-loving people who are proud that their kites fly only in peace. However, because there are no epic stories of Malay kites used in war, their origin is lost.

The earliest written account of Malay kites comes from fifteenth-century chronicles called *Sejarab Melayu*. The story is about the folly of a young prince named Raja Ahmad. During one kite season, the young prince flew a large kite on very strong fishing twine. In a short time, he was able to clear the sky by snipping the twine of any kite that encountered his line. The next day Raja Ahmad repeated the process until he met Hang Isa Pantas's smaller kite. The young prince did not know that Hang had glued powdered glass to his flying twine, using the sap from a jungle tree. When the two lines crossed, the prince's kite line broke and his kite floated away on the wind.

In northern Malaysia, kites are called *wau*. According to a legend from the state of Kedah, the knowledge of how to build the wau began in an effort to appease the heavens. As maintained by the folk story, a farmer and his wife one day found an abandoned baby girl. The couple brought her home and raised her with much love and care and she grew up to be a very beautiful young lady. In time, the farmer loved his adopted daughter more than anything else in the world. His devotion was so great that it provoked the jealousy of his wife to the point that she lost control and beat the girl. Scared, the girl ran for her life and disappeared. From that day forth their farm did not produce a rice harvest and the couple fell into great hopelessness. Not knowing what else to do, they consulted Tok Nujum, a soothsayer. He explained that the girl was in fact the Spirit of the Rice Field, and, as a sign of atonement, the farmer was required to construct and fly a spiritual being in the shape of what is now called a *wau Bulan* ("moon kite"). The farmer did so and in the following year there was a harvest.

Another legend, made famous by the play *Dewa Muda*, tells of how a Malay prince manages to meet his princess, the Spirit of the Spirit King. The young princess lived in the heavens among the clouds and one day threw down flower pebbles from her lofty home, in hopes of meeting her heart's desire. The prince saw the trail of pebbles falling from the sky and was curious to find their origin. He rushed home to the palace, where he begged his mother to allow him to borrow her golden wau. She agreed, and he was able to ride the kite into the heavens and to the arms of his love.

There are many version of how the word *wau* came into being. The most plausible is that it came from the Dutch *wouw*, meaning "a large bird of prey." The northern Malaysian states noted for wau include Kalantan, Terengganu, Kedah, and Perlis. If you visit this region from April to June, you will more than likely witness colorful aerial displays. This is the season of monsoon winds, which are strong enough to fly large kites. It is also a period after the rice harvest when both farmers and deep-sea fishermen have time to celebrate life and good fortune.

On Malaysia's west coast there is used a smaller and less elaborate generic kite called *Layang-layang*. Layang is a Malay word that means "to be borne through the air." During the kite season, local shops do a thriving business selling rice paper, cotton twine, rice glue, and dyes. Along with split bamboo and a winder made from an old coffee can, these materials are all that are needed to make and fly either a child's kite or a fighter kite. However, in many Malaysian states, kite fighting has been banned because it has caused so many disputes among participants.

By removing the tail, the Layang-layang can become a single-line trick kite. To move the kite around the sky, simply nudge on the line until the kite points in the desired direction, and then pull hard on the line. Releasing tension on the line will stop the kite from traveling. It can be tricky at first, but with practice, the kite can be directed all over the sky at the flier's will.

PROJECT 3:
Mini Wau Kite

Recommended for ages 7–12

The Mini Wau Kite is a children's kite meant for flying from a stick and is best flown in light to gentle breezes. Because the wau was a gift from the gods, Malaysians fly them in hopes of good fortune (and fun!) during the monsoon season.

What You Need

SAIL: one 10" (255 mm) x 12" (305 mm) square of light-weight Silkspan or tissue paper

SPARS:

- one 9" (230 mm) x ³⁄₁₆" (4 mm) x ¹⁄₁₆" (2 mm) piece of balsawood, for the spine;
- one 11" (280 mm) x ³⁄₁₆" (4 mm) x ¹⁄₁₆" (2 mm) piece of balsawood, for the top spar;
- two 6" (150 mm) x ³⁄₁₆" (4 mm) x ¹⁄₁₆" (2 mm) pieces of balsawood, for the tail spreaders

PATTERN MATERIAL: heavy paper or cardboard

BRIDLE: this kite has a single tow point with no bridle

BOW LINE: 12" (305 mm) piece of kite line

TAIL: two 1" (25 mm) x 6 feet (2 meter) pieces of tissue or crepe paper

GLUE AND SCRAP PAPER PATCHES

FLYING STICK: one 18" (455 mm) to 24" (610 mm) long plastic balloon straw (available anywhere balloons are sold), or ¼" dowel

KITE LINE: one 24" (610 mm) piece of #10 crochet or buttonhole thread

Making the Kite

1

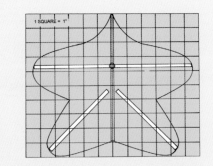

Draw a grid of 1" (25 mm) squares on pattern material. Draw half of the kite sail and cut it out. Mark the location of the spars. Fold the tissue paper in half and trace the pattern onto the sail. Cut out both sides of the kite together.

2

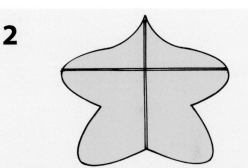

Apply glue along the spine and attach it to the sail. Apply glue along the spars and attach to the sail, using the pattern under the sail to aid in their direction. Glue paper patches over the spine and spar ends.

3

Use a blunt needle to thread the kite line through the sail at the given bridle point. Tie the end of the kite line around the spine and spar.

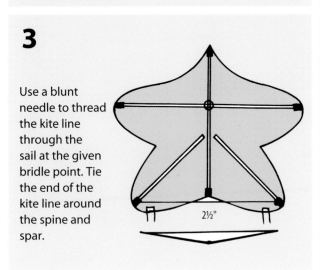

4

Tie a bowline to the ends of the tail spreaders and bow the kite. Glue the tails to the sail. Fly the kite on 2 feet (610 mm) of kite line attached to a balloon straw or dowel.

PROJECT 4:
Layang-layang Kite

Recommended for ages 9–12

This Layang-layang Kite is a good to excellent flier in light to gentle breezes. Malaysian children generally do not use measurements when they make this kite from newspaper and palm fronds or split bamboo. They start with a square sheet of paper, cut spars to fit, and glue it all together with rice paste.

What You Need

SAIL: one 13½" (345 mm) square piece of medium-weight Silkspan

SPARS:
- one 17" (430 mm) x ¼" (6 mm) x ¹⁄₁₆" (2 mm) piece of basswood, for the spine
- one 24" (610 mm) x ¼" (6 mm) x ¹⁄₁₆" (2 mm) piece of basswood, for the spar

BRIDLE: 36" (915 mm) piece of kite line

TAIL:
- one 1" (25 mm) x 6 feet (2 meter) piece of crepe paper for the main tail
- two 1" (25 mm) x 3 feet (1 meter) crepe paper streamers for the side tails

SPAR REINFORCEMENT: one 4" (100 mm) x 1" (25 mm) piece of paper

GLUE AND SCRAP PAPER PATCHES

KITE LINE: #10 crochet or buttonhole thread

Making the Kite

1

Fold the sail in half diagonally. Unfold it and mark the side and bottom flaps. Fold the flaps and crease them. Apply glue along the spine and attach it to the kite. Glue the bottom flap over the spine. Mark the center of the spar and glue the 4" (100 mm) x 1" (25 mm) paper lengthwise around the spar's center.

2

Glue one side of the spar to kite at the corner glue flap. Carefully bend the spar and glue to the other corner flap. You may have to hold the bow for a short time while the glue sets. If the spar is asymmetrical, push down on the high side until both sides are equal. Tape or paste a paper patch to hold the spar in place.

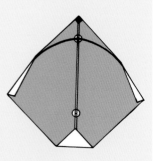

3

Use a blunt needle to thread the bridle through the sail at the given bridle points. Tie the ends of the bridle around the spine and spar at the top bridle point, and the spine at the bottom point.

4

Measure and tie the kite line to the bridle at the tow point. Glue the tails to the kite.

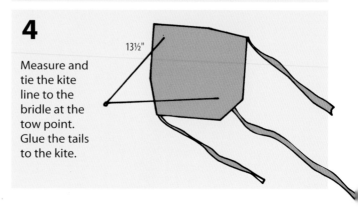

13½"

Kites from Thailand

Kite flying is a very popular pastime in this Southeast Asian country, and kites decorate the sky at the start of the monsoon season. The history of kites in Thailand dates back to the thirteenth century when the country first came into being. There are few written records on the subject, since the sport was handed down from generation to generation through an oral tradition. The earliest documents explain that *ngao* kites were a feature of a ceremony known as *mang*. Priests flew these humming kites—similar to today's *chula*—over the city, either as a form of blessing or in order to predict the weather for the coming season.

During the reign of Phra Phetracha (1688–1703), when the city of Nakhon Ratchasima revolted, the king's army rushed to quiet the rebellion. However, the army had been unable to storm the city by conventional methods, and so they attached long fuses to pots of gunpowder and launched them over the walls. The resulting aerial bombardment set fire to houses, creating enough confusion to enable the soldiers to enter the city and put down the revolt.

Kite flying was not merely a ritual or a part of war; it was a craze enjoyed by everyone from the king down to the common people. It was so popular that kites often became entangled with the roofs of the royal palace, not only damaging buildings but also infringing on the privacy of the monarchy. Eventually the situation became so extreme that a royal edict forbade the flying of kites over the palace.

There is a kite story depicted in a traditional mural at Wat Phra Singh, in the northern city of Chiang Mai. Painted during the reign of Rama V (1868–1910), it tells of a prince who hoped to find a princess to marry by flying a kite and then letting it go. Wherever the kite landed, the prince would seek his bride. The painting shows the kite on the roof of a palace in a distant land and there, at the end of the string, stands a beautiful princess.

Today, there is a kite tradition dating back to when King Rammi II (1809–1892) challenged to match his *chula* against his courtiers' *pakpaos*. The match is a battle of the sexes where the team flying the chula, a large "male" kite, tires to abduct the pakpao, a small "female" kite, while the team flying the pakpao tries to capture the chula. This intricate game makes an exciting sport for the fliers and spectators. In 1921, King Vajiravudh proclaimed this traditional kite game a national sport to be held each March in front of the royal palace. For the first time, both princes and commoners were able to enter their teams and compete for valuable prizes.

For the tournament, a rope divides the flying field. From their upwind positions, the large chulas launch across the border into the downwind half of the field. Here the smaller pakpaos flutter in "swarms like so many butterflies." The chula avoids approaching a pakpao from below, since he is the aggressor and should assume a high and proud position from which he can swoop onto his prey. The pakpao tries to lure the larger kite into an awkward position and then darts across his path, ensnaring him with her tail or loop. Neither kite tries to destroy the other; he tries to abduct her as she tries to capture him.

A chula team has ten to twenty people who work under the direction of a captain. The captain generally controls the team's action by blowing a whistle, but the captain will also take over during critical moments of a catch. In order to make a catch, a flier snaps a brass pulley over the kite line and, to the rhythm of the captain's whistle, the team pulls home the chula with its prey.

When a pakpao succeeds in looping a chula, or if it manages to take the wind out of the larger kite's sail, the chula captain immediately sounds the alarm. At the shrill of the whistle, the chula team makes a final effort to recover their kite and pull it back to the safety of its own territory.

As in northern Malaysia, Thai kites are generally known as *wau*. While the adults participate in their tournament, children enjoy flying kites in the shapes of creatures such as fish, turtles, and cobras.

PROJECT 5:
Thai Cobra Kite

Recommended for ages 9–12

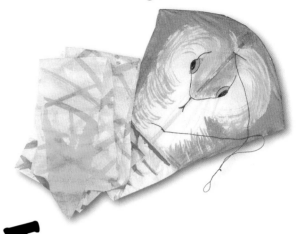

The Thai Cobra Kite is a fair to good flier in gentle to moderate breezes. The long tail adds lift to the kite and acts as a stabilizer; in fact, kiting circles debate how much of the kite is lifting area and how much is stabilizing tail.

In Thai culture, a snake (*naga*) represents the spirit of the snake and dragon, and symbolizes longevity.

What You Need

SAIL AND TAIL: two 24" (610 mm) x 36" (915 mm) pieces of medium-weight Silkspan

SPARS:
- one 14" (355 mm) x ¼" (6 mm) x ¹⁄₁₆" (2 mm) piece of basswood, for the spine
- one 19" (485 mm) x ¼" (6 mm) x ¹⁄₁₆" (2 mm) piece of basswood, for the top spar
- one 7" (180 mm) x ¼" (6 mm) x ¹⁄₁₆" (2 mm) piece of basswood, for the bottom spar

PATTERN MATERIAL: heavy paper or cardboard

BRIDLE: 40" (1115 mm) piece of kite line

TAIL: 10 feet (3 meter) of silkspan or crepe paper tapering down from 7" (180 mm)

GLUE

KITE LINE: #20 kite line (available at kite stores)

Making the Kite

1

Draw half of the kite on the pattern and cut it out. Fold the sail edge wide enough to take the pattern and trace the pattern onto the sail, with the pattern centered along the edge of the fold. Allow a ½" (12 mm) glue flap along the top edge. Cut out the sail and snip at 2" (50 mm) intervals along the glued flap. Apply glue along the spine and attach it to the sail.

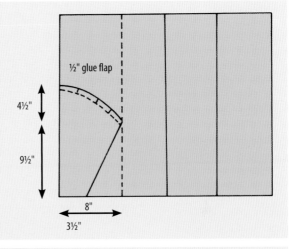

½" glue flap

4½"

9½"

8"

3½"

2

Starting with one top corner, glue the flap over the spar and let the glue set for a moment. Bend the spar and glue the other end to the sail. Finish gluing the rest of the top glued flap. Apply glue along the bottom spar and attach it to the sail.

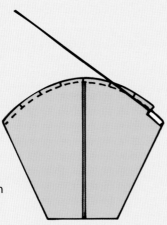

3

Cut the rest of the Silkspan into 7" (180 mm) strips and glue them together to make a 10-foot (3-meter) tail. Glue the tail to the kite and taper to the end. Use a blunt needle to thread the bridle through the sail at the given bridle points. Tie the ends of the bridle around the spine.

4

Measure and tie the kite line to the bridle at the tow point.

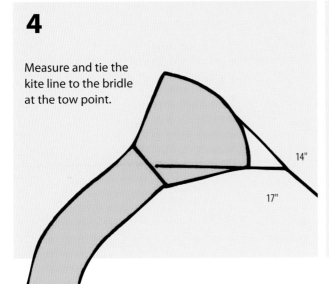

14"

17"

OPTIONAL:
For extra stability, apply white glue to the points where the spars cross.

PROJECT 6:
Thai Fish Kite

Recommended for ages 9–12

The Thai Fish Kite is a fair to good flier in gentle to moderate breezes. In Thailand, fish has been a major source of food for centuries, second only to rice. Because both are associated with water, fish and rice are said to belong together as a pair. In rural farming communities, the rice goddess, who is the great provider of nourishment, is often depicted surrounded by lotus blossoms and fish. The fish represent abundance.

What You Need

SAIL: one 18" (455 mm) x 24" (610 mm) piece of medium-weight Silkspan

SPARS:
- one 18" (455 mm) x ¼" (6 mm) x 1⁄16" (2 mm) piece of basswood, for the spine
- two 14" (355mm) x ¼" (6 mm) x 1⁄16" (2 mm) pieces of basswood, for the top spars
- two 12" (305 mm) x ¼" (6 mm) x 1⁄16" (2 mm) pieces of basswood, for the bottom spars

BRIDLE: 48" (1220 mm) piece of kite line

TAIL: two 2" (50 mm) x 6 feet (150 mm) Silkspan or crepe paper streamers

GLUE AND PAPER PATCHES

PATTERN MATERIAL: heavy paper or cardboard

KITE LINE: #20 kite line (available at kite stores)

Making the Kite

1

Draw half of the kite on the pattern material and cut it out. Draw the spar locations on the pattern. Fold the sail in half and trace the pattern onto the sail, with kite centered along the fold. Cut out the sail.

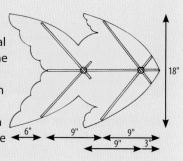

2

Apply glue along the spine and attach it to the sail. Apply glue along the top spars and attach them to the sail, following the pattern under the sail.

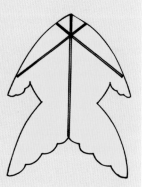

3

Apply glue along the bottom spars and attach them to the sail. Reinforce the sail by gluing patches over the spar ends. Use a blunt needle to thread the bridle through the sail at the given bridle points. Tie the ends of the bridle around the spars and the spine at the bridle points.

4

Measure and tie the bridle to the kite line at the tow point. Glue the tails to the sail.

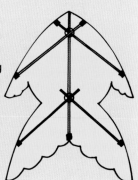

OPTIONAL: For extra stability, apply white glue to the points where the spars cross.

Kites from Korea

Kites in Korea, called *Yeon*, may have arrived from China during the period of the Three Kingdoms (A.D. 4–645), and have changed little over the centuries. As part of national celebrations, people gathered in front of altars to offer yeon as sacrifices to heaven. After such ceremonies, it was customary for people to gather to watch various displays, including kite flying.

One kite-flying story originated during the Silla Dynasty (A.D. 595–673), when General Gim Yu-sin received orders to subdue a revolt, but his troops refused to fight after seeing a falling star, a symbol of imminent disaster. To regain control of his troops, the next evening the general flew a kite with a fireball attached. When the troops saw the "falling star" returning to the sky and disintegrating, they rallied and routed the rebels.

During the Goryo Dynasty (918–1380), General Chue Yung sailed to a rural province by ship to quiet a rebellion. Finding his landing area to be blocked by tall cliffs, the general ordered his men to build large kites and drop fire onto the rebel's stronghold. One account also claims that he landed his soldiers at the top of the cliffs with the aid of kites.

Yongzo, the twenty-first king of the Yi Dynasty (1392–1910), once lamented the lack of kite flying in his kingdom. He asked a minister if there was something wrong, since his people had not been enjoying kite flying during the past several years. The story of the king's concern quickly spread across the kingdom and soon there were many kites flying across the country.

The Korean kite-flying season closely relates to the agricultural cycle. People once refrained from flying kites during the farming season out of fear of damaging the crops. Koreans begin flying kites on *seollal*, the first day of the lunar calendar. After paying a New Year's visit to their elders, relatives, and neighbors, both children and adults fly kites. The kite season lasts for fifteen days, or until the first full moon of the year. The annual Korean custom also involves kite fighting. The tradition also includes the flying of special kites, named *aeg-mag-i-yon* or *song-aeg-yon*, on the fifteenth day or soon afterward. These kites can ward off evil, and they are made by writing on an ordinary kite these words: *Bad luck away and good luck stay*. Traditionally, the flier will release the line when the kite reaches the end of its tether. In this fashion, the kite supposedly carries away the owner's bad luck, and children are discouraged from retrieving such a freed kite, since it may possess evil spirits.

Kites are also flown on *chuseok*, the Korean day of giving thanks. At the end of a kite season, Korean custom once dictated that kites could not fly again until the following year.

In 1954, the Minister of Culture and Tourism opened a kite competition, the first one since South Korea proclaimed independence. The ultimate form of Korean kite flying is kite fighting, which is exciting to both spectators and fliers.

The winning flier is generally the one with the sharpest line and best technique. Once cut from its kite line, the freed kites belong to whomever can capture them. Koreans do not attach blades to their kites; instead they rely on their specially prepared line to do the cutting.

The Korean fighter kite is called a *bang-pae-yeon* ("shield kite"). This kite is unique because of its rectangular shape and central circular vent, called a *bang-gu-mong*. It is a semi-stable flier when flown tailless in aerial combat. Either the individual fliers or professional artisans make Korean fighters from mulberry paper and bamboo. The size of the kite will depend on the area's wind strength. In strong wind areas, such as near the sea, kites need to be large, with thick spars and a two-ply paper sail.

PROJECT 7:
Shield Kite

Recommended for ages 9–12

The Shield Kite is a good flier in gentle to moderate breezes. This traditional Korean fighting kite is named for the color and type of decoration. For example, a *hong-ggog-zi* is a kite with a red circle (representing a moon) on its central "head," or top of the kite. Here are some other types of Shield Kite:

> *ggog-zi*: has a whole circle on the central head;
> *mog-ban-dal*: has a half-circle on the central head;
> *dong-l*: has a belt on the "forehead" or "waist";
> *gwi-mo-ri-zang-gun* (big corner hair and ear kite): has a two-colored triangle at each top corner
> *gu-ri-pal-gwae-yon*: has eight horizontal stripes and a full moon on the central head.

These kites use the colors *hwang* (yellow), *chong* (blue), *mog* (black), *bo-ra* (purple), *gum* (gold), and *hong* (red).

What You Need

SAIL: one 15" (380 mm) x 21" (535 mm) piece of medium-weight Silkspan

SPARS:
- one 20" (510 mm) x ¼" (6 mm) x ¹⁄₁₆" (2 mm) piece of basswood, for the spine
- one 15" (380 mm) x ¼" (6 mm) x ¹⁄₁₆" (2 mm) piece of basswood, for the top spar
- one 14" (355 mm) x ¼" (6 mm) x ¹⁄₁₆" (2 mm) piece of basswood, for the center spar
- two 24" (610 mm) x ¼" (6 mm) x ¹⁄₁₆" (2 mm) pieces of basswood, for the cross spars

PATTERN MATERIAL: one 6" (150 mm) circle pattern, such as a dish

BRIDLE: three 23" (585 mm) pieces of kite line

BOWLINE: kite line

TAIL: one 2" (50 mm) x 10 feet (3 meter) crepe paper streamer

FEET: two triangular paper patches

GLUE

KITE LINE: #20 kite line (available at kite stores)

Making the Kite

1

Fold a ½" (12 mm) glue flap along each side (the 21" edge) and glue. Fold a 1" (25 mm) glue flap along the top edge, but do not glue it yet. Fold the sail in half in both directions. Draw a 6" (150 mm) circle in the center and cut it out.

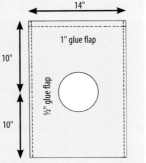

2

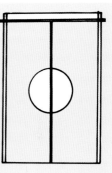

Apply glue along the top spar and attach it to the sail. The spar should overhang each side. Apply glue along the spine and attach it to the sail.

3

Apply glue along the cross spars and attach them to the sail. The top of the spars should extend ½" (12 mm) above the sail. Apply glue along the center spar and attach it to the sail. Now you may glue down the top glue flap.

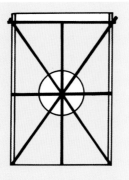

4

Tie the bridle to the spars at both top-corner bridle points, and tie a bridle leg to the spars and around the spine at the central bridle point. Glue the triangular feet to the bottom corners of the sail and attach the tail. Tie the bowline at both ends of the spar. Carefully bow the spar, and wind any excess line around the end of the spar.

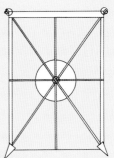

5

Measure and tie the kite line to the bridle at the tow point.

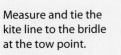

OPTIONAL:
For extra stability, apply white glue to the points where the spars cross.

PROJECT 8:
Ray Fish Kite

recommended for ages 9–12

The Ray Fish Kite is a fair to good flier in light to gentle breezes. This rhombus-shaped kite resembles a stingray in the sky and is typical of children's kites that exist all over Asia; it is called a *tenbata* in Japan, a *pillian* in China, and layang-layang in Malaysia. The bowed cross spar helps to stabilize the kite in moderate breezes by bending to the wind's pressure.

What You Need

SAIL: one 13½" (345 mm) square piece of medium-weight Silkspan

SPARS:
- one 19" (485 mm) x ¼" (6 mm) x ¹⁄₁₆" (2 mm) piece of basswood, for the spine
- one 21" (535 mm) x ¼" (6 mm) x ¹⁄₁₆" (2 mm) piece of basswood, for the spar

BRIDLE: this kite has a single tow point with no bridle

TAILS:
- one 2" (50 mm) x 8 feet (2.5 meter) strip of Silkspan, for the main tail
- two 5" (130 mm) x 3½" (90 mm) triangular pieces of tissue paper, for the side fins

GLUE AND 2" (50 MM) PAPER PATCHES

KITE LINE: #10 crochet thread

30

Making the Kite

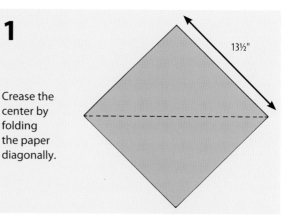

1 Crease the center by folding the paper diagonally.

13½"

2 Apply glue along the spine and attach the sail along the crease. Reinforce the sail by gluing paper patches over the spine ends.

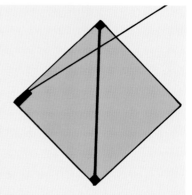

3 Apply glue to a paper patch and use it to attach one end of the spar to the sail at one corner. Bow the spar and glue the other end to the opposite corner with a paper patch. Use a blunt needle to thread the bridle through the sail, at the point where the spine and spar cross, and tie the line end around the spine and the spar.

4 Glue the side fins and the tail to the kite.

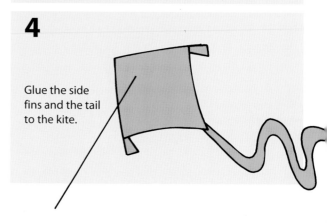

Kites from Japan

Japanese civil servants brought the knowledge of making kites and paper to Japan from China during the seventh century. Kites held a position of such importance and prestige in Japan that only the privileged classes and Buddhist monks could fly them. The monks used kites as talismans to keep evil spirits away and to invoke a rich harvest. The Japanese also consider a kite to be an object to carry petitions to the spirit gods, called kami. Furthermore, there is a traditional Japanese belief that a destroyed kite's soul is released and is free to be reborn in another kite.

Shien, meaning "paper hawk," was the first word written to describe Japanese kites, and it occurred in the book *Wamyou ruiju sho* from the Heian Period (794–1185). Over the following centuries, many Japanese folk stories involving kites were written, but the tales of the use of kites in war and to lift men in amazing feats are questionable at best. In the twentieth century, members of the Shirone Kite Battle Association tested the theory of a man-carrying kite, but were not able to prove the feasibility of using large kites for such a purpose.

The popularity of Japanese kites reached a high point during the Edo Period (1603–1868), when they were embraced by both the privileged and lower classes. Not surprisingly, kites became so popular that the government tried unsuccessfully to outlaw them when too many people became "unmindful of their work." From Edo, kites made their way to the provinces as souvenirs and became the basis for the development of many of Japan's distinctive designs, some with symbolic importance. There are approximately 340 different traditional kites made in Japan in forty-two districts. Most Japanese call kites tako, but in different regions other names are often used,

such as *hata* ("flag") in Nagasaki, *ika* ("squid") in Niigata, and *tenbata* in Miyagi.

Japanese families today continue to share the essence of their heritage through kites on special days such as *O-Shogatsu* (New Year's Day) and *Kodomo-no-hi* (Children's Day, on May 5). Children receive kites decorated with folk heroes, creatures, or gods in the hopes that they will obtain strength, vigor, and a prosperous life. However, some of today's small kite gifts are meant only as tokens because they do not actually fly.

Kintaro, one of Japan's folk heroes, is often depicted on kites wrestling with a bear or carp. He was born and raised in the Ashigara Mountains in Kanagawa and enjoyed animals as his playmates. Japanese parents give Kintaro kites to their children in the hopes that they will grow as healthy and courageous as their champion. In the northern Japanese town of Hachinohe, there once lived a painter who would paint petitions to a local god at a Shinto shrine. He would paint a picture of his patron's request and leave it at the shrine. One day a woman asked if he could paint a kite with a picture of Kintaro so that her son would grow up to be big and strong. Puzzled by the request, the painter asked the woman what she was going to do with the kite. She explained that since the gods lived in the heavens she wanted her message to go directly to them instead of waiting for the deities to visit the shrine. When the story spread around town, others made similar requests for kites.

In Miyagi, families used to make small *tenbata* kites bearing their names. On New Year's Day, the kites were flown in the nearby mountains and the lines cut. It was believed that the freed kites would take away all evil, assuring a prosperous new year.

One of the most recognized Japanese traditions occurs in May during "Golden Week," with the flying of *koinobori* from bamboo poles. Westerners often mistake these carp windsocks for kites, but the windsocks cannot fly like kites because their shape does not create lift. In the wind, the carp appear to be swimming vigorously against the current, symbolizing strength and fortitude. The top windsock represents flowing water, a large black carp represents the father figure, a smaller red carp is for the mother, and each smaller carp below represents a child in the family.

Not all Japanese kite festivals are geared toward children, though many of the adult events are dedicated to the firstborn. During Golden Week, kite battles take place at Hamamatsu, Sagara, and Ikazaki; during June, teams battle with kites in Sanjo and Shirone. Also during Golden Week, teams of Japanese challenge the elements with giant kites at Sagamihara, Showa-machi, Yokaichi, and Zama.

PROJECT 9:
Octopus Kite
Recommended for ages 7–12

The Octopus Kite is a fair to good flier in gentle to moderate breezes. The Octopus Kite comes from Sanjo, in Niigata, on Japan's west coast. The Japanese name, Tako-no-tako, is a play on words: *Tako* means both "octopus" and "kite." During the Edo Period, kite makers often suspended these octopus-shaped kites in front of their stores as a sign of their occupation.

What You Need

SAIL: one 8" (205 mm) x 12¼" (310 mm) piece of medium-weight Silkspan

SPARS:
- one 11" (280 mm) x ¼" (6 mm) x ¹⁄₁₆" (2 mm) piece of balsawood, for the spine
- two 8" (205 mm) x ¼" (6 mm) x ¹⁄₁₆" (2 mm) pieces of balsawood, for the spars

BRIDLE: 36" (915 mm) piece of line

TAIL: one 4¾" (120 mm) x 24" (610 mm) piece of medium-weight Silkspan

GLUE AND PAPER PATCHES

KITE LINE: #10 crochet thread

Making the Kite

1

Draw the whole kite sail on the pattern material and cut it out. Mark the location of the spars on the pattern. Trace the pattern onto sail and cut out the sail.

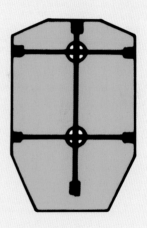

2¼" 3½" 2¼"

2"

5½"

3¼"

1"

7¾"

3½"

4½"

2

Fold the sail in half to help locate where to glue the spine. Apply glue along the spine and attach it to the sail along the fold.

3

Apply glue along the spars and attach them to the sail, using the pattern under the sail as a guide. Glue paper patches over the ends of the spars.

4

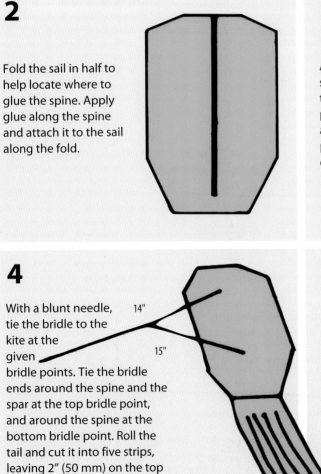

With a blunt needle, tie the bridle to the kite at the given bridle points. Tie the bridle ends around the spine and the spar at the top bridle point, and around the spine at the bottom bridle point. Roll the tail and cut it into five strips, leaving 2" (50 mm) on the top uncut. Glue the tail to the sail.

14"

15"

OPTIONAL:
For extra stability, apply white glue to points where the spars cross.

PROJECT 10:
Bug Kite

Recommended for ages 7–12

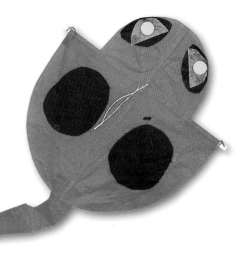

The Bug Kite is a fair flier in gentle to moderate breezes. The Bug Kite takes its shape from a beetle; many Japanese children keep large beetles as pets because they live in small homes and there is little space for animals.

What You Need

SAIL: one 10" (255 mm) x 12" (305 mm) piece of tissue paper

SPARS:
- one 12" (305 mm) x ¼" (6 mm) x ¹⁄₁₆" (2 mm) piece of balsawood, for the spine
- one 11½" (mm) x ¼" (6 mm) x ¹⁄₁₆" (2 mm) piece of balsawood, for the top spar
- two 3" (75 mm) x ¼" (6 mm) x ¹⁄₁₆" (2 mm) pieces of balsawood, for the spreaders

PATTERN MATERIAL: heavy paper or cardboard

BRIDLE: this kite has a single tow point with no bridle

BOWLINE: one 14" (35 mm) piece of kite line

TAIL: one 5-foot (1.5 meter) x 1½" (40 mm) paper streamer

GLUE

KITE LINE: #10 crochet thread

Making the Kite

1

Draw half of the kite sail on the pattern material and cut out the sail. Fold the tissue paper in half and trace the pattern onto sail. Cut out both sides together, allowing for a 1" (25 mm) glue flap along the top edge.

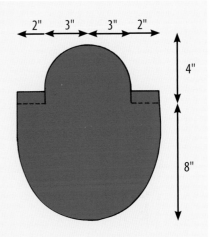

2

Apply glue along the spine and attach it to the sail. Apply glue along the top spar and attach it to the sail. Glue the two flaps over the spar.

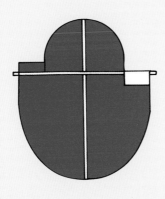

3

Using a blunt needle, tie the kite line to the kite at the point where the spar and spine cross, and tie a line end around the spine and spar. Tie the bowline to the ends of the spar, carefully bow the kite, and wind any excess line around the ends of the spar.

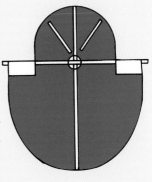

4

Halfway up the tail, split the tail in two, and glue it to the sail.

OPTIONAL:
For extra stability, apply white glue to the points where the spars cross.

PROJECT 11:
Buka Fighting Kite

Recommended for ages 7–12

T he Buka Fighting Kite is a good flier in gentle to moderate breezes. The Buka comes from Mori and Iwata, in Shizuoka, in central Japan. This kite was named because the larger versions are said to make a *buka-buka* sound as they fly skyward. The Buka first flew during the Edo Period to honor the newborn son of Lord Tsuchiya Sado-no-kami.

What You Need

SAIL: one 20" (510 mm) x 15" (380 mm) piece of medium-weight Silkspan

SPAR:

- one 14" (355 mm) x ¼" (6 mm) x ¹⁄₁₆" (2 mm) piece of basswood, for the spine
- one 20" (510 mm) x ¼" (6 mm) x ¹⁄₁₆" (2 mm) piece of basswood, for the top spar
- two 24" (610 mm) x ¼" (6 mm) x ¹⁄₁₆" (2 mm) pieces of basswood, for the cross spars

BRIDLE: 40" (1115 mm) piece of kite line

BOWLINE: 22" (560 mm) piece of kite line

TAIL: two 5-foot (1.5 meter) x ½" (12 mm) paper streamers

GLUE AND PAPER PATCHES

KITE LINE: #10 crochet thread

Making the Kite

1

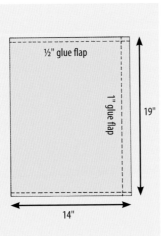

Fold a ½" (12 mm) glue flap along each side (the 15" [380 mm] edges) and glue. Fold a 1" (25 mm) glue flap along the top edge, but do not glue it yet.

½" glue flap

1" glue flap

19"

14"

2

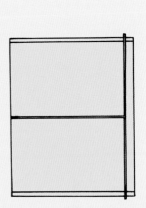

Apply glue along the top spar and attach it to the sail. The spar should overhang each side. Apply glue along the spine and attach it to the sail.

3

Apply glue along the cross spars and attach them to the sail. The top of the spars should extend ½" (12 mm) above sail. Glue down the top glue flap and glue the paper patches over the spars along the bottom edge.

4

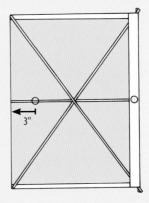

Using a blunt needle, tie the bridle to the kite at the given bridle points. Tie the bridle ends around the spine. Measure and tie the kite line to the bridle at the tow point.

3"

5

Tie the bowline at both ends of the spars. Carefully bow the spars and wind any excess line around the ends of the spars. Glue the tails to the sail.

16"

18"

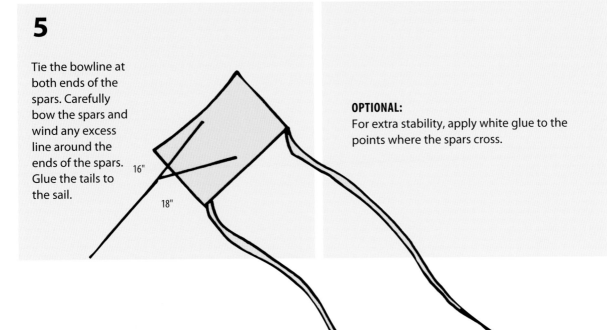

OPTIONAL:
For extra stability, apply white glue to the points where the spars cross.

Spinning-top Kite

Recommended for ages 7–12

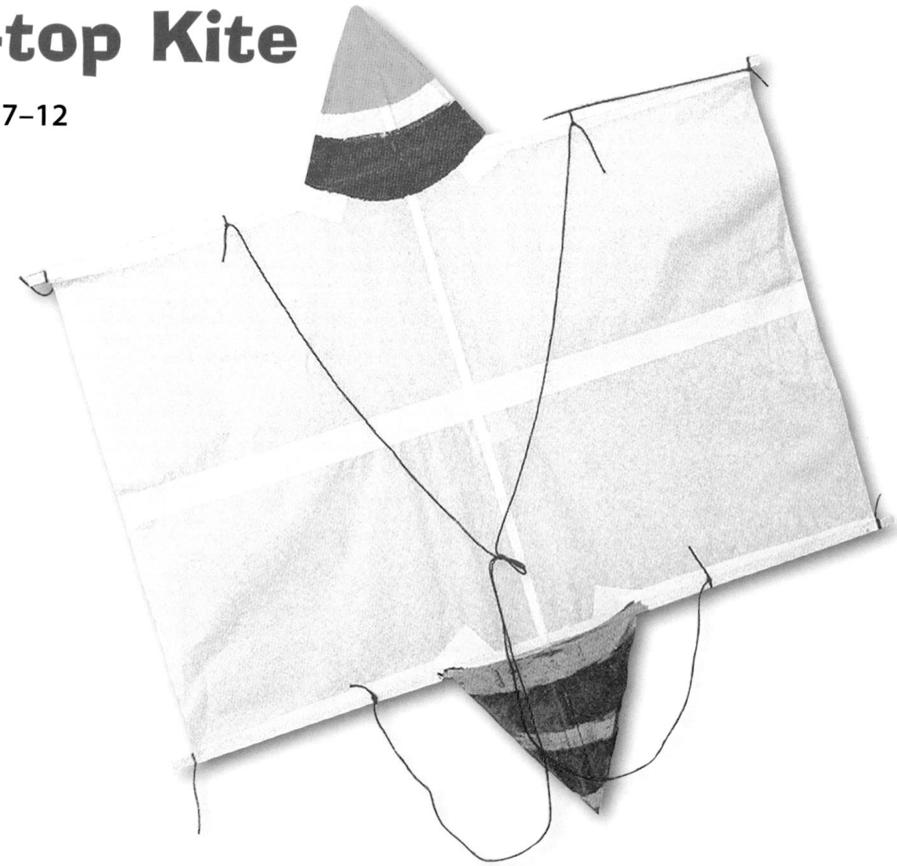

T he Spinning-top Kite is a good to excellent flier in gentle to moderate breezes. This kite represents a child's spinning-top toy, and it is generally flown tailless. Spinning-top Kite are made in central Japan in Iwatsu (in Saitama), Yonezawa (in Yamagata), and Tokyo.

What You Need

SAILS:
- one 15" (380 mm) x 20" (510 mm) piece of medium-weight Silkspan
- two 5" (130 mm) x 5" (130 mm) triangular pieces of medium-weight Silkspan, for the top and bottom sails

SPARS:
- one 22½" (570 mm) x ¼" (6 mm) x ¹⁄₁₆" (2 mm) piece of basswood, for the spine
- two 21" (535 mm) x ¼" (6 mm) x ¹⁄₁₆" (2 mm) pieces of basswood, for the cross spars

BRIDLE: two 34" (865 mm) pieces of kite line

BOWLINE: two 24" (610 mm) pieces of kite line

TAIL: optional

GLUE

PAPER PATCHES: two large triangular pieces

KITE LINE: #10 crochet thread

Making the Kite

1

Fold ½" (12 mm) glue flaps along the top and bottom ends (the 20" [510 mm] sides). Unfold the flaps. Fold the sail and two triangular ends in half to locate the center. Glue the pieces together. Snip along the edge of the top and bottom triangles so the glue flap can fold.

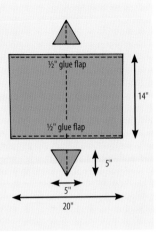

2

Apply glue along the spine and attach it to the sail. Glue the triangular paper patches over the ends of the spine.

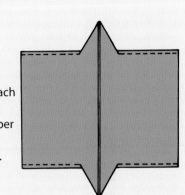

3

Apply glue along the spars and attach them to the sail. Glue down the glue flaps.

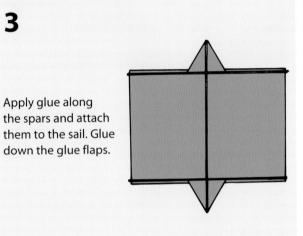

4

Using a blunt needle, tie the bridle to the kite at the four given bridle points. Tie the bridle ends around the spars.

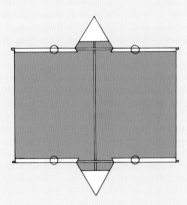

5

Measure and tie the kite line to the bridle at the tow point. Tie the bowline to the spar ends. Bow the kite and wind any excess line around the ends of the spars.

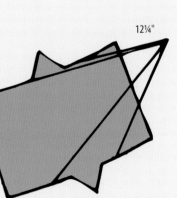

OPTIONAL:
For extra stability, apply white glue to the points where the spars cross.

PROJECT 13:
Six-sided Kite

Recommended for ages 10–12

The Six-sided Kite is an excellent flier in gentle to moderate breezes and it is one of only a few Japanese kites that can roll up for storage. Six-sided Kite come mainly from Niigata, where they are known as *maki-ika* ("rolled squid"). Larger versions play an important part in aerial battles each June in the towns of Shirone and Sanjo. The Sanjo Six-sided Kite is said to have originated when the townspeople one day tried to cut down the kite of a *samurai* (a Japanese warrior) with their own rectangular kite. In retaliation, the samurai cut off the corners of his antagonists' kite, thus creating this six-sided kite. Six-sided Kite are traditionally painted with pictures of folk heroes, warriors, and Kabuki actors.

What You Need

SAIL: one 24" (610 mm) x 28" (710 mm) piece of medium-weight Silkspan

SPARS:
- one 29" (735 mm) x ³⁄₁₆" (4 mm) dowel, for the spine
- two 24" (610 mm) x ¼" (6 mm) x ⅛" (3 mm) pieces of spruce, for the cross spars

PATTERN MATERIAL: heavy paper or cardboard

BRIDLE: two 60" (1530 mm) pieces of kite line

FRAMING LINE: piece of kite line

BOWLINE: two 28" (710 mm) pieces of kite line

TAIL: this kite is tailless

GLUE AND PAPER PATCHES

KITE LINE: #20 kite line (available at kite stores)

Making the Kite

1

Draw half of the kite sail on the pattern material, allowing for ½" (12 mm) glue flaps along each edge, and cut it out. Fold the sail in half and trace the pattern with the kite centered on the fold. Cut out both sides of the sail at the same time. Unfold the sail and fold the glue flaps, but do not glue them yet.

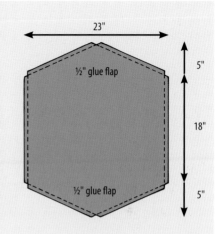

23"

½" glue flap

½" glue flap

5"

18"

5"

2

Apply glue along the cross spars and attach them to the sail. Start gluing the framing line under the glue flaps, and tie the framing around the spars as you go. Finish with approximately 3" (75 mm) of line at the bottom. Cut a slot at each end of the dowel (spine) and fit the dowel into the framing line at the top of the kite. Tie the ends of the framing line around the bottom of the spine. Note that the spine is removable, so you can roll the kite. Reinforce the stress points and bridle points by gluing paper patches onto them.

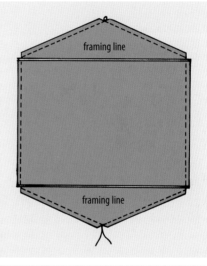

framing line

framing line

3

Using a blunt needle, tie the bridle to the spars at the four given bridle points. Tie the bridle ends around the spars.

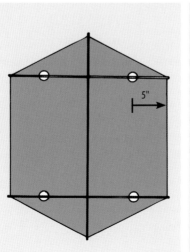

5"

4

Measure and tie the kite line to the bridle at the tow point. Tie the bowlines across the spar ends. Bow the kite, and wind any excess line around the ends if the spars.

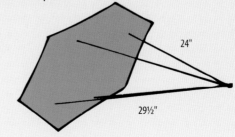

24"

29½"

PROJECT 14:
Kite from Suruga

Recommended for ages 10–12

T he Kite from Suruga is an excellent flier in gentle to moderate breezes. Kite from Suruga are made in Shizuoka and Nagaizumi, in Shizuoka, in central Japan. In the early sixteenth century, after a minor battle, Imagawa Yoshimoto, the lord of Suruga Castle, asked one of his servants fly a Kite from Suruga over the castle as a sign of victory. Kite from Suruga are traditionally painted with the faces of folk heroes, warriors, and Kabuki actors.

What You Need

SAIL: one 21" (535 mm) square of medium-weight Silkspan

SPARS:

- one 20" (510 mm) x ¼" (6 mm) x ¹⁄₁₆" (2 mm) piece of basswood, for the spine
- one 16" (405 mm) x ¼" (6 mm) x ¹⁄₁₆" (2 mm) piece of basswood, for the top spar
- two 24" (610 mm) x ¼" (6 mm) x ¹⁄₁₆" (2 mm) pieces of basswood, for the cross spars

PATTERN MATERIAL (OPTIONAL): 21" (535 mm) x 15" (380 mm) piece of heavy paper or cardboard

BRIDLE: three 40" (1 meter) pieces of kite line

BOWLINE: 20" (510 mm) piece of kite line

TAIL (OPTIONAL): paper streamers

GLUE AND PAPER PATCHES

KITE LINE: #20/30 kite line (available at kite stores)

Making the Kite

1

Draw and cut off a 3" (75 mm) x 7-½" (190 mm) triangle at each bottom corner of the pattern and tape them to the sides. Trace the pattern onto the sail with the kite centered on the fold and cut it out. Fold a 1" (25 mm) glue flap along the top edge, but do not glue the flap yet.

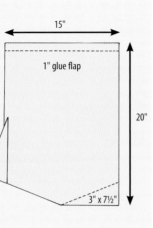

15"

1" glue flap

20"

3" x 7½"

2

Apply glue along the top spar and attach it to the sail. The spar should overhang each side. Apply glue along the spine and attach it to the sail. The spine should overhang the bottom.

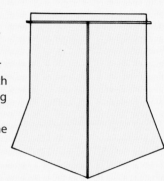

3

Apply glue along the cross spars and attach them to the sail. The tops of the spars should extend approximately ½" (12 mm) above the sail.

4

Glue down the top glue flap and glue paper patches over the spars, along the bottom edge. Using a blunt needle, tie the bridle to the kite at the given bridle points. Tie the bridle ends around the spine.

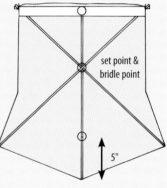

set point & bridle point

5"

5

Hold the bridle together at the set point. On this particular kite, the set point happens to fall at the point where the cross spars intersect. Move your hand along the bridle and tie a loop at the end, creating a tow point. Tie a third leg from the set point to the tow point. Tie a bowline and bow the spar 2½" (65 mm). Wind any excess line around the spar end.

OPTIONAL:
For extra stability, apply white glue to points where the spars cross.

PROJECT 15:
Sleeve Kite

Recommended for ages 10–12

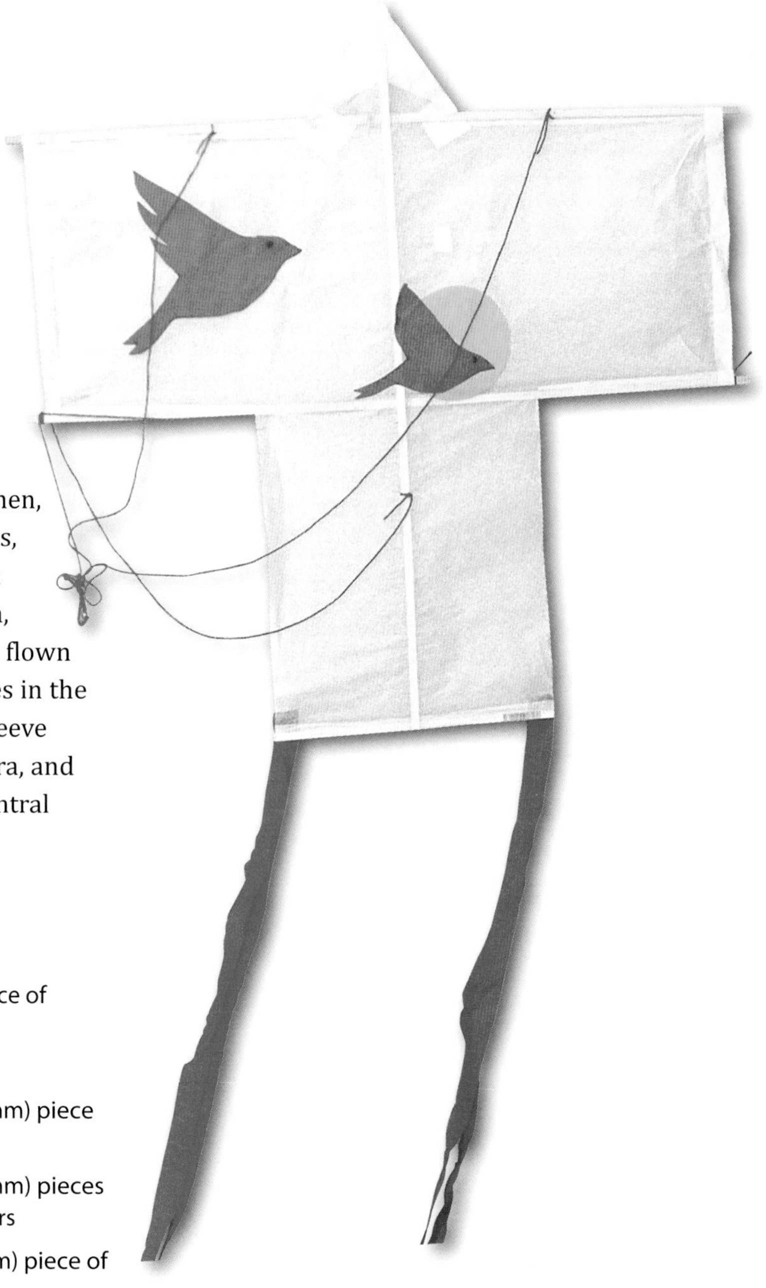

The Sleeve Kite is an excellent flier in gentle to moderate breezes. The Sleeve Kite evolved around 1780 when, in celebration of a large catch of sardines, someone made a kite from a celebration coat, called a *happi*. From this time forth, fishermen from Chiba have traditionally flown Sleeve before setting sail on long voyages in the hopes of a safe and successful return. Sleeve Kite are made in Honno, Mobara, Ichihara, and Ichinomiya on the Boso Peninsula, in central Japan.

What You Need

SAIL: one 24" (610 mm) x 24½" (620 mm) piece of medium-weight Silkspan

SPARS:

- one 24" (610 mm) x ¼" (6 mm) x 1/16" (2 mm) piece of basswood, for the spine
- two 24" (610 mm) x ¼" (6 mm) x 1/16" (2 mm) pieces of basswood, for the top and center spars
- one 9" (230 mm) x ¼" (6 mm) x 1/16" (2 mm) piece of basswood, for the bottom spar

PATTERN MATERIAL: heavy paper or cardboard

BRIDLE: three 40" (1 meter) pieces of kite line

BOWLINE: two 20" (510 mm) pieces of kite line

TAIL (OPTIONAL): paper streamers

GLUE AND PAPER PATCHES

KITE LINE: #20/30 kite line (available at kite stores)

Making the Kite

1

Draw half of the kite sail onto the pattern material, allowing ½" (12 mm) glue flaps, and cut out the sail. Trace the pattern onto the sail with the kite centered on the fold, and cut it out. Fold the glue flaps, but glue only the side flaps.

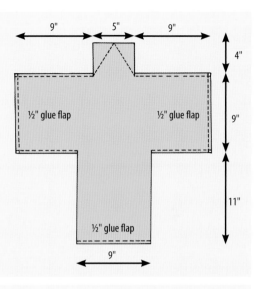

9"   5"   9"

4"

½" glue flap   ½" glue flap

9"

11"

½" glue flap

9"

2

Apply glue along the spine and glue it to the kite. Diagonally fold top section and glue it over the spine. Apply glue along the bottom spar and glue it to the kite. Glue the flap over the spar. Apply glue along the cross spars and attach them to the sail. Glue the glue flaps over the spars. The spars should extend approximately ½" (12 mm) beyond the sail. Reinforce the stress points and the given bridle points with paper patches. Using a blunt needle, tie two bridle legs to the kite at the two bridle points along the top spar, and tie to the spine at the third bridle point.

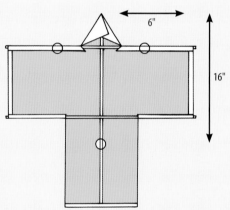

6"

16"

3

Measure and tie the kite line to the bridle at the tow point. Tie the bowline, bow the spars approximately 3" (75 mm), and wind any excess line around the spar ends.

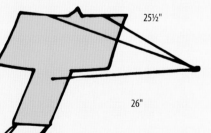

25½"

26"

OPTIONAL:
For extra stability, apply white glue to points where the spars cross.

Kite Workshops
A Note for Parents and Teachers

Making Asian kites is an excellent way to study other cultures in the classroom, especially when the activity is combined with showing a video and world map to illustrate the place where they originated.

Depending on the class's ability and size, it is often advisable for the teacher to make the patterns for the kite and even precut the sails and spars. The teacher should also make and test fly the kite before the class meets. The teacher's kite will also make an excellent example for the class. Perhaps the teacher could make or purchase several types of kites to hand around the classroom so that the students can have a better understanding of their constructions.

With a medium to large class size, I recommend that two students work on one kite together. The students can decorate their own creations before going outside to fly their kites.

For large classes, I use 3" (75 mm) x 5" (130 mm) foam-core board for line winders, as cardboard tends to collapse. To wind the line, the students take turns running out their line and then cutting it to the desired length. Each student then winds the line onto his or her winder. Foam-core board is available from craft and art supply stores.

If the class is studying a particular culture, such as Japanese, and the teacher wants to be as true as possible to the culture, than it is advisable to have samples of actual Japanese kite art to copy. A Japanese master allows a student to trace his work until the student is proficient enough to paint a kite on his or her own. I learned in Japan that it can take an apprentice two years to learn to paint an eye! My Japanese kite teacher had such art blown up so that I could trace the design on my sail with charcoal before painting the kite. Kite pictures can be blown up to the desired size with a photocopier. Windows make excellent light tables for tracing the design. Alternatively, you can project the image onto a wall for the students to trace.

For group workshops, it is advisable to have all materials precut, and set up stations to create an assembly line.

Online Resources

Kite Materials and Suppliers

Goodwinds.com: Kiting Supply
https://goodwinds.com

Great Winds Kite Co.
www.kiteguys.ca

Hang-Em High Fabrics
www.kites.tug.com

Into the Wind
intothewind.com

Kite Studio Converter
www.kitebuilder.com

Michaels Arts and Crafts
www.michaels.com

SIG Manufacturing Co., Inc.
www.sigmfg.com

Kite Associations and Museums

American Kitefliers Association
www.aka.kite.org

Japanese Kite Association
www.tako.gr.jp

World Kite Museum
kitefestival.com

Bibliography

Barwell, Eve, and Conrad Bailey. *How to Make and Fly Kites*. London: Studio Vista, 1974.

Brummitt, Wyatt. *Kites*. New York: Golden Press, 1971.

Bushell, Helen. *Make Mine Fly*. East Kew: Australian Kite Assoc., 1987.

Dyson, John, and Kate Dyson. *Fun with Kites: How to Make Eighteen Beautiful Kites*. London: Angus and Robertson, 1976.

Fowler, H. Waller. *Kites: A Practical Guide to Kite Making and Flying*. New York: A.S. Barnes, 1953.

Greger, Margaret. *Kites for Everyone*. Richland, WA: M. Greger, 1984.

Ha, K'uei-ming, and Yigi Ha. *Chinese Artistic Kites*. San Francisco, CA: China Books & Periodicals, 1990.

Hart, Clive. *Kites: An Historical Survey*. New York: Praeger, 1967.

Hiroi, Tsutomu. *Kites: Sculpting the Sky*. New York: Pantheon Books, 1978.

Hosking, Wayne. *Fighter Kites and Beyond*. Clermont, FL: Skytec, 2000.

———. *Kites of Japan*. Clermont, FL: Skytec, 2000.

———. *Kites*. New York: Friedman/Fairfax Publishers, 1994.

———. *Kites of Malaysia*. Kuala Lumpur: Malaysian Airline System, 1990.

Ito, Toshio and Hirotsuga Komura. *Kites*. Tokyo: Japan Publications, 1979.

Jue, David F. *Chinese Kites: How to Make and Fly Them*. Rutland, VT: C.E. Tuttle Co., 1967.

Moulton, Ron. *Kites*. London: Pelham, 1978.

Mouvier, Jean Paul. *Kites*. Paris: Collins, 1974.

Musa bin Jusoh, Wan. *Wau Malaysia*. Belia dan Sukan, Malaysia: Kementerian Kebudayaan, 1976.

Newman, Lee Scott, and Jay Hartley Newman. *Kite Craft: The History and Process of Kitemaking Throughout the World*. New York: Crown Publishers, 1974.

Pelham, David. *The Penguin Book of Kites*. New York: Penguin Books, 1976.

Spaulding, Ron, et al. *Thailand's Chula and Pakpao Kites*. Bangkok: Thai Kite Heritage Group, 2002.

Streeter, Tal. *The Art of the Japanese Kite*. New York: Weatherhill, 1974.

Sang-su, Ch'oe. *The Survey of Korean Kites*. Seoul: Korea Books Pub. Co., 1958.

Thomas, Bill. *The Complete World of Kites*. Philadelphia: Lippincott, 1977.

Wagenvoord, James. *Flying Kites*. New York: Macmillan, 1968.

Yolen, Will. *The Complete Book of Kites and Kite Flying*. New York: Simon and Schuster, 1976.

Published in 2005 by Tuttle Publishing, an imprint of
Periplus Editions (HK) Ltd.

www.tuttlepublishing.com

Library of Congress Control Number: 2017946308
ISBN 978-0-8048-4930-2

Distributed by

North America, Latin America & Europe
Tuttle Publishing
364 Innovation Drive
North Clarendon, VT 05759-9436
Tel: (802) 773-8930; Fax: (802) 773-6993
info@tuttlepublishing.com
www.tuttlepublishing.com

Japan
Tuttle Publishing
Yaekari Building, 3rd Floor
5-4-12 Osaki Shinagawa-ku
Tokyo 141 0032
Tel: (03) 5437-0171; Fax: (03) 5437-0755
sales@tuttle.co.jp
www.tuttle.co.jp

Asia Pacific
Berkeley Books Pte. Ltd.
61 Tai Seng Avenue #02-12
Singapore 534167
Tel: (65) 6280-1330; Fax: (65) 6280-6290
inquiries@periplus.com.sg
www.periplus.com

20 19 18 17   10 9 8 7 6 5 4 3 2 1   1708RR
Printed in China

Diagrams by Wayne Hosking
Illustrations by Masturah Jeffrey

TUTTLE PUBLISHING® is a registered trademark of
Tuttle Publishing, a division of Periplus Editions (HK) Ltd.

ABOUT TUTTLE
"Books to Span the East and West"

Our core mission at Tuttle Publishing is to create books which bring people together one page
at a time. Tuttle was founded in 1832 in the
small New England town of Rutland, Vermont
(USA). Our fundamental values remain as strong
today as they were then—to publish best-in-
class books informing the English-speaking
world about the countries and peoples of Asia.
The world has become a smaller place today
and Asia's economic, cultural and political influence has expanded, yet the need for meaningful
dialogue and information about this diverse
region has never been greater. Since 1948,
Tuttle has been a leader in publishing books on
the cultures, arts, cuisines, languages and litera-
tures of Asia. Our authors and photographers
have won numerous awards and Tuttle has published thousands of books on subjects ranging
from martial arts to paper crafts. We welcome
you to explore the wealth of information available on Asia at **www.tuttlepublishing.com**.